Mangoes & Bullets

John Agard

Mangoes & Bullets

Selected and new poems 1972–84

SERPENT'S
TAIL

First published 1985 by Pluto Press, London
The Works, 105a Torriano Avenue, London NW5 2RX
and Pluto Press Australia Limited, PO Box 199, Leichhardt,

Shoot Me With Flowers first published in 1973 by John Agard; *Man to Pan* first
published in 1982 by Casa de las Americas; *Limbo Dancer in Dark Glasses* first published
in 1983 by John Agard, Greenheart.

'My Telly' reproduced from the collection *I Din Do Nuttin*
by kind permission of the Bodley Head

This edition published 1990 by
Serpent's Tail, 4 Blackstock Mews, London N4

Phototypeset by AKM Associates (UK) Ltd
Ajmal House, Hayes Road, Southall, Greater London

Printed in Great Britain by
The Longdunn Press, Bristol

British Library Cataloguing in Publication Data
Agard, John
   Mangoes & bullets : selected and new poems
   1972–84.
   I. Title
   811   PR320.A1

ISBN 1 85242 124 X

Contents

Himself Interviews Himself

An introduction by the author

Himself: First of all, do you prefer to be addressed as a palm tree king, a weatherman, or an instructor in the art of eating mangoes?

Himself: I will need to give that question some thought. I am cautious of labels.

Himself: Well, can you tell us briefly about the collections from which some of these poems were taken?

Himself: My first collection, *Shoot Me With Flowers*, was self-published in 1973 back in Guyana. Flower culture had a late brief bloom in Guyana and these poems go back to a time when Viet Nam, the Beatles, Black Power and Peace & Love were part of our consciousness. The poems in *Shoot Me* grow out of that mood and the intimacy of a personal relationship. Wasnt easy plucking poems from that book/they belong to a wholeness.

Himself: Your next collection, *Man to Pan*, celebrates the evolution of Steelband, a cycle of poems to be performed with drums & steelpans. Did you yourself do much writing and performing between *Shoot Me With Flowers* in 1973 & *Man to Pan* in 1982?

Himself: Yes, I had three children's books published, two here and one in Guyana, but before leaving home I had some unpublished poems, mostly about Guyanese street characters, and a few creole stories for radio. By 1975, I had joined up with the All-ah-We, a mobile group of Guyanese actors/raconteurs: Ken Corsbie, Marc Matthews, Henry Mootoo. I also did a short spell of performing poems with a jazz group in a nightspot in Georgetown. Being with the All-ah-We taught me a lot about audience involvement, which comes out in my later work.

Himself: *Man to Pan* was awarded the 1982 Cuban Casa de las Americas Poetry Prize. This literary competition has been open to Latin American writers for more than 20 years and is now open to writers from the entire Caribbean. Is it true that you were also offered an honorary knighthood from the Society Against Stereotypes?

Himself: That's only a rumour. Don't believe a word of it.

Himself: This brings us to your migration to the UK in 1977. I gather that your trip was uneventful apart from your luggage being searched for explosive mangoes. Six years later you were to produce *Limbo Dancer in Dark Glasses*. Is there any logical connection between these events?

Himself: If there is, it is sheerly subconscious. The Limbo Dancer sequence took off from a traditional view that limbo dancing was born in the cramped conditions of the slave ship/a far cry from the tourist image.

Himself: To describe your performing style you use the word poetsonian, and the Jamaican poet Mervyn Morris observed that your body language is akin to that of the calypsonian. Do you agree with this?

Himself: Yes, I like how he put it. But I also got in mind a kinship with the satirical spirit & folky surrealism of the calypsonian. Who else but a calypsonian would like to reincarnated as a bedbug? Who else but a calypsonian would conceive of a district magistrate trying his own case ('himself charge himself for contempt o' court') and giving himself five years to pay a fine of 20 dollars? The whole resurgence of the oral art in poetry has caused black poets to come up with words of their own making. You can think of jazzoetry/Gil Scott-Heron calls himself bluesician or bluesologist/you also got dub poetry, using reggae beat/rapso poetry/& a number of white poets call themselves ranters. Not that anything is wrong with the word poet. Is just that most people have come to see 'poet' & 'poetry reading' in very distant cerebral terms. So using these other terms I just mentioned is like subverting the expectations of audiences. Is a way of reclaiming other art forms into poetry like theatre & not treating poetry as isolated. So Ntozake Shange, for instance, describes her work as choreopoem or poemplay/incorporating dance & drama/and I describe a long children's poem I did recently, growing out of different musical instruments, as a poemsemble. It's nothing new really, it's a return to ancient traditions, a return to the troubadour & the shaman/shawoman.

Himself: One final question. What do you miss most about the Caribbean?

Himself: I miss sweating.

Dedication

Remembering Walter Rodney & Maurice Bishop
two of our Caribbean dream-doers
               &
for CLR James square-cutting ideas in his 80s
for John LaRose with affection
for Marc Ken & Henry of the All-ah-We
               &
for Grace companera sculpting long-memories beside me
for my mother Anna De Souza
who made sucking mango a fine art

Thanks from de weatherman
to Mandy Williams of Apples & Snakes
& Pete Ayrton of Pluto Press
two quiet villains behind the piece

From
Shoot Me With Flowers (1973)

shall we walk in or turn back?

For My Daughter Yansan

At two minutes past six
you screamed your wombsong coming
into a new world
of shape and sound

what brings you to these shores little one?
what dreams lie curled
in this your feathersoft fist
she who mothered you can never tell

what pains will touch your path
between the cradle and the grave
no one knows

but like the flower that grows
knowing not which wind
will one day uncomb its bloom
so must you my child

so sleep well little one
and dream your dream
before the price of sleep becomes too dear

For All Who Fell in Wars Within and Without the Heart of Man

The butterfly
above his head
made the sleeping soldier
think the enemy was near

bullets rained upon the earth
and flowers were exiled from their stems

bombers scarred the sky with fear
and birds migrated into their wings

gases flooded death into the sea
and fishes got up on their fins and prayed

and men with guns growing out their hands
were too afraid to touch how frail each other was

when flowers catch bullets in the wind
and napalm deflowers the dawn
let one soldier become a child again
and make his gun a reed
for butterflies to rest on

when machine gun baby screams
in the cradle of fire
let one soldier become a child again
and fill his helmet with grasses
for sparrows to nest in

when shrapnel blossoms spring
in the path of the yellow reaper
let one soldier become a child again
and with his bayonet write the words
of buddha in the sand

when tank fires burn the lips of wind
and earth tosses in sleep
let one soldier become a child again
and making of his tank a plough
furrow the land for new seed

when the world bleeds with the voice of my lai
and hiroshima falls upon the cheeks
let one soldier become a child again
and pitching his bullets into the sky
watch them wheel like birds that cause no pain

Rationalization Does Not Reach the Ecstasy of Things

(something marilyn said back in '72)

I remember
you told me
rationalization
does not reach
the ecstasy of
things
and my brain
stammered
in your hands'
caress
and my ideas
limped deeper
into the skull
and my logic
shrivelled
in your sixth sense
and my mind
menstruated
endless
abstractions
not feeling
the moon
between your thighs
and my flesh sang
in your flower
presence
and my bone
became soft enough
for you to pierce
with petals
and I love you
woman
for becoming and
moving
myself
to essence

Waiting for Fidel

(on the occasion of the visit of Fidel Castro, 2 September 1973,
Timehri Airport, Guyana)

The cubana bird touched down
tore the blanket of heat
from around the taut faces
waiting
for a slice of history

a people starved of freedom
and hungry for heroes

then suddenly there you stood
breath of the sierra maestra
proud as tall green cane

you could have been a lover
come home from a long journey

but now something disturbs our sleeping guts
something close to pain

and an untouchable sadness
turns like a key
in the door of history

shall we walk in or turn back?

From **Man To Pan** (1982)

Hammerblows on metal are actsoflove
but listen well for tones of rage and hurt

Journey Shango

On new ground we scatter old drum seeds
letting them shape a destiny of sound
unburdening the iron in our blood.
Thunder roots new voice in steel
and lightning seams metal with song.

Who would have dreamed that Shango heart
would beat this far would follow us
across strange water to stranger earth
rising to thunder from oildrum rust?

Deliver

DELIVER
hammer
blows
on steel/
DELIVER
steel
belly
groan/
DELIVER
steel
skin
stretch/
DELIVER
steel
flesh
shudder/
DELIVER
steel
womb
pulse
& burn/
DELIVER
till
birth
cry
of steel
mudder
say
PAN
borNN
PraisSSEE GoddDD

Web of Sound

is the sinking

is the cleaving

is the weaving

is the sounding

is the drumming

is the grounding

is the pounding

is the wounding

is the grooving

is the moving

of metal

of a feeling

of a dream

of a scream

of a heart

of a hurt

of a rage

of a night

of blackness

of a man

of pan

for the taste of fire

to the thrust of chisel

in a web of sound

in old oildrum

to a beat of steel

to tones of blood

to tunes of love

by slash of stars

by trickles of light

to the embrace

Flight of Fingers

Flight of fingers
flight of wingtip rubber
through a landscape of grooves
through a limbo of steel

Fly panman fly
you know this skyline web
of hummingbirdsound
like the palm of yuh hand

Fly?

Fly?
It ain always so easy
to fly above slum/mess
even with wings of tenderness

It ain always so easy
to break out this damn prison
of history
even with instruments of reason

wrench this slave/shadow/chain
clinging like bad/blood
in the basin of mih memory

The weight of centuries heavy.
Man, I up to mih neck in scars

But black night mek for stars
and stars born to shine

So when you see me caressing steel
you must know I hold the dream of pan
to ease the itch/and switch/of knifeblade

For Hands Honed

For hands honed by pan grooves
hammerblows on metal are actsoflove
but listen well for tones of rage and hurt

Watch that miracle of sound flow
from hands attuned to mystery of steel.
Bloodriddum tells him what is real

In oildrum darkness
watch them hands chisel notes like stars well/seamed
temper rustgloom to pan tuner's dream

Yes, hammerblows on metal are actsoflove
but listen well for tones of rage and hurt

Heap of History

Is more than a snapshot mirror
reflecting panman face
in a mood of concentration
complete with perspiration

Is more than a straw/hat/native
making a merry steel show
whilst he catching ass to live
in some bad/john/ghetto

Is more than knocking out a tune
on a sunbeach/package/tour
with rum flowing like blood
and the body calling for more

No/
pan deeper than that man
                    is a heap of history in you hand

I Cant Hear You Man

When I crouch over
with mih head inside a pan
no use talking to me man
cause I ain't hearing/
Mih ear too full-up
with the sound of lightning
tearing
darkness into splin/
ters/
Is Shango fingers
playing havoc with mih brain
No use talking to me man
when I crouch over
with mih head inside a pan
The whispers
I hearing
is the softer side of thunder
Know wha ah mean?
And if you wonder
where ah been
well I making a rounds
of the heavens
watching God full-eye
through circle rims of light
that could pass for metal
in the dark
if you not seeing right/
Now I turning down
a side street
of a night
name history
and if you can't see me
just follow the panbeat
and you won't go wrong
but don't blame me pardner
if you get loss
cause mystery is pan father
like spider web self/
No use calling out mih name

I cant hear you man
not when I crouch over
with mih head inside a pan/
Now ah following
spider footstep
across the water
dodging
like Midnight Robber
with steelsound
for mih dagger
and the only gun
ah carrying
is O/gun
dream of iron
on new ground/
So you could brandish
yuh whip
how much you wish
if you think you go see me slip
you got to think again
cause Shango thunder
binding whipcrack
to a stammer
and history
is a bitch
I go lavish
with flowers of steel
till she memory
mesmerize with sound
and she wish
she ship
did run a/ground
But too late
too late is the cry
and these rims
of darkness ·
leaking light
from mih eye
is more than rings

of pain
or lack of sleep/
Is a long deep
moving
to a/wakening
a hurtful growth
And I got to hold the birth
of vision
hold the birth
of vision
springing
from this web
of steel
singing
from the depth
of night
till ah feel
earth
move with love
groove with light
and after centuries
of turning

mih back to the sun
burning like whip
in mih memory
ah learning
to embrace
another sun
with rays
of melody
under me/
so no use talking to me man
when I crouch over
with mih head inside a pan
cause I aint hearing/
Mih head inside the sun
and the water
searing
the rim
of mih eye
is no ordinary sweat/
Is Shango sweating fire
to a kiss of steel

Rain of Sounds

In a rain of sounds
rebounding
from belly to brain
in a rain of sounds
unbound
by shanty/town
or history/wounds
steelpan
steelpain
steelrage
steelsweetness
unchain
a rain of sounds
and watch
rusting memories
drown

Beat It Out

Beat it out man
beat out the hurt
beat it out
to riddum of steel/
feel
panblood flow
watch the dream
grow
from things unshaped
to real/
beat it out man
beat it out
beat out the rape
of the whip
shadow
the burn and blow
on gaping skin/
beat it out man
beat it out
beat out the weight
of history
scar/and/hate

beat it out man
beat it out
beat out the bleed
and spill
of seed
to waste/
beat it out man
beat it out
beat out
a new message
from de middle/
passage
womb of riddle/
beat it out man
beat it out
beat out the burden
of history
sound
beat it/heal it/shape it
confound
wounds
with vision

From
Limbo Dancer in Dark Glasses (1983)

whether male or female
who can be sure

who can pin a gender
on this limbo dancer

who can dare decipher
this human spider

dismembered under
a deck of fire

Limbo Dancer's Wombsong

From timeless waters
of the primal womb
I was dancing soon

believe me it was fun
in the primal womb
like great balloon

though my limbs were tender
I'd bend backwards over
giving a mighty quiver

sometimes I'd stretch umbilical cord
like an extra limb
& revel dancing under

such sweet contractions
my mother said she felt
she wanted to carry me forever

Rainbow

When you see
de rainbow
you know
God know
wha he doing –
one big smile
across the sky –
I tell you
God got style
the man got style

When you see
raincloud pass
and de rainbow
make a show
I tell you
is God doing
limbo
the man doing
limbo

But sometimes
you know
when I see
de rainbow
so full of glow
and curving
like she bearing child
I does want know
if God
ain't a woman

If that is so
the woman got style
man she got style

Limbo Dancer & the Press

The western press never took kindly
to limbo dancer gyrations

described by one paper as deadly
to international relations
hazard to territorial integrity

With head perched in the highlands of Guyana
knees spread wide in Venezuela

neck arched somewhere in Argentina
toes touching Falklands

hands cleaving chill Afghanistan air
legs bent bowlike across USSR

limbs doing frenzied to & fro
between Southern Africa and Lesotho

and when limbo dancer cried in Namibia
a limbo of tears descended in Soweto

Cynics called this a cheap acrobatic stunt
the western press cried Soviet propaganda

From the Kremlin there was no comment at first
but things really got worse
when limbo dancer rippled under
Berlin Wall to applause of tourists

To the Soviets this was no acrobatic stunt
this was bourgeois and decadent

No one thought of calling limbo dancer
simply a child of the universe

The Reason

Because they know
I have centuries of bending behind me

because they know
I can bend so low
barbed wire cannot hold me

they felt a concentration camp
would not be safe enough for me
and though six million Jews did not agree

they decided to send me to Chile
and there they held me facedown in a stadium

I thought they would have smashed my knees
as they did Victor's hands
instead they simply called me missing

But because they know
I have centuries of bending behind me

they felt a stadium
would not hold me for very long

so they transferred me to Southern Africa
where I was placed in solitary confinement
but it was the same in that other continent

I thought they would have manacled my ankles
as they had done with Biko

But because they know
centuries ago
I had learnt to live with manacles

they decided to banish me
to a living hell
and the name of Mandela rang a bell

But because they were told
they had got the wrong man/or the wrong woman

since to them my sex was indecipherable
and in any case unimportant

and knowing I was capable of a million disguises

they gave the order to shoot on sight
without question
anything seen bending backwards

so if you should see anywhere
a rifle aimed towards the rainbow

you must know
I limbo dancer

am the reason

Limbo Dancer's Mantra

LIMB/BOW
Pronounce dem
two syllable
real slow
you hear me
real slow

LIMB/BOW
Savour dem
two syllable
till glow
spread from head
to tip of toe

LIMB/BOW
Contemplate dem
two syllable
in vertigo
of drum tempo

LIMBO
Meditate on dem
two syllable
calm as zero
vibrate to sound
let mind go

and forget the stick
I tell you
don't think about the stick

that will take care of itself

Limbo Dancer's Reading Habits

Limbo dancer reads The Wretched of the Earth
bending over backwards

Limbo dancer reads How Europe Underdeveloped Africa
bending over backwards

Limbo dancer reads Che Guevara's diary
bending over backwards

Limbo dancer reads Angela Davis' autobiography
bending over backwards

Limbo dancer reads Capitalism and Slavery
bending over backwards
and has chained every word to memory

But limbo dancer also reads the Kama Sutra
bending over backwards
as well as The Joys of Natural Childbirth

Some believe this is what make limbo dancer
capable of sustaining multiple revolutions

Out of the Question

Once in my life I did make a blunder
when one psychiatrist looked at me with wonder
and said I don't care if your name is limbo dancer
that couch is not meant for dancing under

Besides you dance like one inviting copulation
and that for me is quite out of the question

Take a Tip

Here's news for all you lovers

not to bruise each other
with games of ego

but to fuse each other
with flames of limbo

to lose self in sweet surrender

take a tip from one
who like water
has danced under
many bridges of time

From **Palm Tree King** (1983)

don't expect me to be brief
cause palm tree history
is a long-long story

Palm Tree King

Because I come from the West Indies
certain people in England seem to think
I is a expert on palm trees

So not wanting to sever dis link
with me native roots (know what ah mean?)
or to disappoint dese culture vulture
I does smile cool as seabreeze

and say to dem
which specimen
you interested in
cause you talking
to the right man
I is palm tree king
I know palm tree history
like de palm o me hand
In fact me navel string
bury under a palm tree

If you think de queen could wave
you ain't see nothing yet
till you see the Roystonea Regia
– that is the royal palm –
with she crown of leaves
waving calm-calm
over the blue Caribbean carpet
nearly 100 feet of royal highness

But let we get down to business
Tell me what you want to know
How tall a palm tree does grow?
What is the biggest coconut I ever see?
What is the average length of the leaf?

Don't expect me to be brief
cause palm tree history
is a long-long story

Anyway why you so interested
in length and circumference?
That kind of talk so ordinary
That don't touch the essence
of palm tree mystery
That is no challenge
to a palm tree historian like me

If you insist on statistics
why you don't pose a question
with some mathematical profundity?

Ask me something more tricky
like if a American tourist with a camera
take 9 minutes to climb a coconut tree
how long a English tourist without a camera
would take to climb the same coconut tree?

That is problem pardner
Now ah coming harder

If 6 straw hat
and half a dozen bikini
multiply by the same number of coconut tree
equal one postcard
how many square miles of straw hat
you need to make a tourist industry?

That is problem pardner
Find the solution
and you got a revolution

But before you say anything
let I palm tree king
give you dis warning
Ah want de answer in metric
it kind of rhyme with tropic
Besides it sound more exotic

Stereotype

I'm a fullblooded
West Indian stereotype
See me straw hat?
Watch it good

I'm a fullblooded
West Indian stereotype
You ask
if I got riddum
in me blood
You going ask!
Man just beat de drum
and don't forget
to pour de rum

I'm a fullblooded
West Indian stereotype
You say
I suppose you can show
us the limbo, can't you?
How you know!
How you know!
You sure
you don't want me
sing you a calypso too
How about that

I'm a fullblooded
West Indian stereotype
You call me
happy-go-lucky
Yes that's me
dressing fancy

and chasing woman
if you think ah lie
bring yuh sister

I'm a fullblooded
West Indian stereotype
You wonder
where do you people
get such riddum
could it be the sunshine
My goodness
just listen to that steelband
Isn't there one thing
you forgot to ask
go on man ask ask
This native will answer anything
How about cricket?
I suppose you're good at it?
Hear this man
good at it!
Put de willow
in me hand
and watch me stripe
de boundary

Yes I'm a fullblooded
West Indian stereotype

that's why I
graduated from Oxford University
with a degree
in anthropology

English Girl Eats Her First Mango

(a kind of love poem)

If I did tell she
hold this gold
of sundizzy
tonguelicking juicy
mouthwater flow
ripe with love
from the tropics

she woulda tell me
trust you to be
melodramatic

so I just say
taste this mango

and I watch she hold
the smooth cheeks
of the mango
blushing yellow
and a glow
rush to she own cheeks

and she ask me
what do I do now
just bite into it?

and I was tempted
to tell she
why not be a devil
and eat of the skin
of original sin

but she woulda tell me
trust you to be
mysterious

so I just say
it's up to you
if you want to peel it

and I watch she feel it
as something precious

then she smile and say
looks delicious

and I tell she
don't waste sweet words
when sweetness
in you hand

just bite it man
peel it with the teeth
that God give you

or better yet
do like me mother
used to do
and squeeze
till the flesh
turn syrup
nibble a hole
then suck the gold
like bubby
in child mouth
squeeze and tease out
every drop of spice

sounds nice
me friend tell me

and I remind she
that this ain't
apple core
so don't forget
the seed
suck that too
the sweetest part
the juice does run
down to you heart

man if you see
the English rose
she face was bliss
down to the pink
of she toes

and when she finish
she smile
and turn to me

lend me your hanky
my fingers
are all sticky
with mango juice

and I had to tell she
what hanky
you talking bout
you don't know
when you eat mango
you hanky
is you tongue

man just lick
you finger
you call that
culture
lick you finger
you call that
culture

unless you prefer
to call it
colonization
in reverse

Wanted Man (New Poems)

I warning you Mr Oxford don
I'm a wanted man
and a wanted man
is a dangerous one

Immigrant Neighbours

What do you do
when your immigrant neighbours
slaughter a sheep
in view of the street

Downright cruelty
It doesn't matter
if the sheep
has got diplomatic
immunity

It's a cause for concern
it's a cause for lament
a matter for parliament
where's our bloody MP

An all-night party
with all-night jungle music
can at worst disturb our sleep
but the cry of a sheep
can bring down the value
of our property
Besides it just isn't a nice thing to do
Not in front of the children

A video nasty
now that's a different matter
our little ones just love to see
a monster's blood spatter
but the neck of a sheep
and just a few feet from our front garden!

Religious did you say
ritualistic!
Why can't these foreigners
be more like us
why can't they act civilized
and organise a decent fox hunt
why don't they go to the countryside
and shoot squirrels
that pester our trees
whey don't they try
some squirrel and kidney pie

but surely not a sheep I ask you
that isn't our idea of a barbecue!

Listen Mr Oxford don

Me not no Oxford don
me a simple immigrant
from Clapham Common
I didn't graduate
I immigrate

But listen Mr Oxford don
I'm a man on de run
and a man on de run
is a dangerous one

I ent have no gun
I ent have no knife
but mugging de Queen's English
is the story of my life

I dont need no axe
to split/ up yu syntax
I dont need no hammer
to mash/ up yu grammar

I warning you Mr Oxford don
I'm a wanted man
and a wanted man
is a dangerous one

Dem accuse me of assault
on de Oxford dictionary/
imagine a concise peaceful man like me/
dem want me serve time
for inciting rhyme to riot
but I tekking it quiet
down here in Clapham Common

I'm not a violent man Mr Oxford don
I only armed wit mih human breath
but human breath
is a dangerous weapon

So mek dem send one big word after me
I ent serving no jail sentence
I slashing suffix in self-defence
I bashing future wit present tense
and if necessary

I making de Queen's English accessory/to my offence

Finders Keepers

This morning on the way to Charing Cross
I found a stiff upper lip
lying there on the train seat

Finders Keepers
I was tempted to scream

But something about that stiff upper lip
left me speechless

It looked so abandoned so unloved
like a frozen glove
nobody bothers to pick up

I could not bear to hand in
that stiff upper lip
to the Lost & Found

So I made a place for it
in the lining of my coat pocket

and I said
Come with me to the Third World

You go thaw off

Cowtalk

Take a walk to the splendid morning fields of summer
check out the cows in full gleam
of their black and white hide

and remember was a man once say I have a dream
but they shoot him down in cold blood of day
because he had a mountaintop dream
of black and white hand in hand

take a walk to the splendid morning fields of summer
check out the cows in green of meditation
a horde of black and white harmony

maybe the cows trying to tell us something
but we the human butchers cant understand cowtalk
much less cowsilence
to interpret cowsilence you must send for a poet
not a butcher or a politician

cows in the interwoven glory
of their black and white hide
have their own mysterious story
cows in the interwoven glory
of their black and white hide
never heard of apartheid
never practise genocide
never seem to worry
that the grass greener on the other side
cows calmly marry and intermarry

cows in the interwoven glory
of their black and white hide
cows in the interwoven glory
of black and white integration
cant spell integration
cows never went to school
that's why cows so cool supercool
cows have little time for immigration rule
and above all cows never impose
their language on
another nation

do yoo moo my message/do yoo moo
moo my message/moo
do yoo moo my message/do yoo moo
moo my message/moo

Weatherman

I am de weatherman
and dere's no dreaderman
in English company
than de weatherman
and dat's me

I am de weatherman
de ghost at every conversation
rising higher than inflation
de shadow across your day
controlling your destiny
with visions of grey

I am de weatherman
I come dancing out of thin air
to send my chilly breath
down the reaches of your ear and neck
and dere's nothing your thermal vest
could do about it you hear

I am de weatherman
your friendly prophet of doom
de eternal conversation piece
but occasionally I make room
for football results and British Leyland

I am de weatherman
standing back with professional ease
smiling a sweet 2 degrees
below zero smile
because I'm a sadist at heart
and enjoy watching you freeze

I am de weatherman
grinning behind scattered showers
de mastermind of atmosphere
and my allies are everywhere
neatly dressed invisible powers
disguised as that fellow passenger
who never ever remembers
to close a train door
that thoughtful person
with one eye on the skies
who always carries an umbrella
just in case
just in case
just in case

I am de weatherman
and like the phoenix I rise
from the foggy ashes
of the 9 o'clock news
proclaiming my northwesterly blues
so better get our your non-slip shoes

I am de weatherman
de sore thumb in your diary
de frosty finger on your spine
because I'm allergic to sunshine

I am de man
to make de taxman
tremble for a taxfree touch of sun
I am de man
to make President Reagan
reach for his gun
I am de man
to make de Iron Lady
reach for her cardigun

Yes I am de weatherman
and dere's no dreaderman
no dreaderman
no dreaderman

Rag and Bone

The rag and bone man
is always ready for romance
the rag and bone man
will do a dance
in a heap of rubbish
the rag and bone man
is a dreamer
who will keep a blind date
with an old vacuum cleaner
the rag and bone man
will sweep you off your feet
on a magic carpet
studded with precious dust
the rag and bone man
will unburden his lust
in the arms of a warped sofa
the rag and bone man
is someone you can trust
if you have no junk to throw out
then give him your heart
the rag and bone man
will keep it warm
under a broken lampshade

Anancy's Thoughts on Love*

Love got teeth
as old people say
dont know if you walking
on you hand or you feet
but it dont really matter
cause you bound to meet
sooner or later

love is watching hint
big and bold
but refusing to catch it

love is trapping thoughts
in side-eye gaze
long before thoughts see light-of-day

love is sweet mystery
like sleight-of-rain

But love is sweet misery
like taste-of-pain

love is going down winding labyrinth
at loss for words
and loss of head
but Anancy thank God
always have piece of thread
for way back out

or to put it another way
Anancy in love
always save back piece of heart
for peace of mind

---

* Anancy is a trickster spider man figure traditional to Caribbean folk tales

Tough Guy

There's a tear trying to tiptoe
towards the edge of your eye tough guy
there's a tear leaning
in the direction of your eye
towards the rim of your eye tough guy

What's the matter tough guy

Why do you push it down
with the palm of your ego

A tear wouldn't bruise your eyelid

Maybe tough guy when you were a kid
they told you little boys dont cry
Didn't you ever see your Daddy peeling onions?

Your hands can talk to steel and batteries
but cant bear to deal
with the weight of a leaf

Tough luck tough guy
have a good cry

Go Garlic

america going garlic
it's true it's true
havent you heard yet
america passing thru
the garlic phase
man it's the latest craze
the new american dream

garlic toffee
garlic sweeties
garlic cookies
garlic icecream
you might think I'm lying
but health freaks buying
garlic t-shirts
that say GO GARLIC   *audience repeat:* Go garlic
and garlic flirts
giving each other the garlic come-on

badges of the 60s
that said MAKE LOVE NOT WAR
have given way
to badges of the 80s
that say GO GARLIC   *audience repeat:* Go garlic
GARLIC IS MAGIC

garlic it's true
is good for you
the healing properties
go back to ancient times
when garlic didn't cost a dime
and old socrates might
have craved a feg or two
the garlic pearls of wisdom

but gee whiz man
you gotta give it to america
when america does something
america does it big you dig
wanna be fit
      GO GARLIC   *audience repeat:* Go garlic
wanna be hip
      GO GARLIC   *audience repeat:* Go garlic
worried bout your dick
      GO GARLIC   *audience repeat:* Go garlic
wow the garlic revolution
gonna take your breath away

that is
if a nuclear bomb dont
get you first

My Telly★

My telly eats people
especially on the news.

Little people
with no shoes
Little people
with no food
Little people
crying
Little people
dying.

My telly
eats people
If you don't
believe me
look inside
the belly
of my telly.

★ From John Agard's collection of poems for children, *I Din Do Nuttin*

Unemployment May Be High
But You Can't Blame
the Advertising Industry
for Not Taking Stock
of the Ethnic Minority

Nobody noticed him
He was an alien
in a strange white

        world

until he smiled
his ethnic smile

        ULTRA-BRITE

a flash
of ivory
in the dark
of night

Think right
Get ethnic
Buy ULTRA-BRITE
tonight

UNEMPLOYMENT MAY BE HIGH
BUT YOU CAN'T BLAME
THE ADVERTISING INDUSTRY
FOR NOT TAKING STOCK
OF THE ETHNIC MINORITY

For kiddies
who like teddies
shreddies
and golliwogs

from Kelloggs
organically grown cobs
comes a breakthru
in breakfast special

        KELLOGGS BCF
        KELLOGGS BLACK CORN FLAKES

it's new
it's authentic
it's organic
it's special

Savour the flavour
in a startling colour

Be fair to your kids
help them start their day
the multi-racial way

Miss Lou* on Stage at the Commonwealth Institute, London 1983

Watch she when she squinch-up she eye
another laugh coming out she headtie
but old people sey not every skinteeth is laugh/
is mock de lady mocking she mocking
and de audience dem rocking dey rocking

Dem dont want dis concert end
dem want carry home dis legend
like beads of boonoonoonoos words/
dis pride in mudder language giver
dis lady who could sing in C
but prefer to sing in river

Anyway de lady seh she tired. 'Me tired'
and who to know if she tongue in she mouth or she cheek
de audience dem want more
remember she is sixty-four
though she still girlish with labrish charm
'Me tired'

But dont bother tell she goodbye/tell she walk good
walk good Miss Lou walk good Miss Lou/
me hope good duppy follow you

---

* Louise Bennett, a legendary performer and pioneer of Jamaican creole in
poetry

Heart Transplant

No puff
no pant
check out
a heart transplant

let's swop
your heart
for mine
heart transplant
the new life line

come on baby do the heart transplant
come on baby do the heart transplant

experiment number 1
put the heart of a bird
inside a stone
meditate on that

behold
the stone sings
the stone grows wings
wondrous flight
of a common thing

experiment number 2
a medical breakthru
put the heart of your average politician
into a common stone

behold
stones grow paranoid
stones grow suspicious of grass
stones hurl themselves into the void
the blue emptiness

alas
will stones develop a paunch

seeking the votes of God

Child Waiting

(for lesley)

little head
at the window
in childeyed wonder

the ceaseless
come and go
of mighty traffic
must be moving magic
to your unblinking gaze

but how patient
are eyes looking for one
named mummy
in a rumble of wheels

Poems from 'Let Our Rivers Meet'

(a love cycle for grace)

learning to swim

learning to swim
    you surrender
    your woman's body

            limb
            by cautious limb

    to the cool
    embrace
    of water
        in a pool
            until
    kicking
    your feet
    like wayward fins
you discover anew
that ancient foetal sense

            and wait
            for innocence
            to drown you

mole

it was always there
that mole
on the nape of your neck
delicate
in its nest of hair

but somehow
discovering it today
as if for the first time
reminds me all the more
that like the land
our bodies
yield their treasures
where least we seek

One Question from a Bullet

I want to give up being a bullet
I've been a bullet too long

I want to be an innocent coin
in the hand of a child
and be squeezed through the slot
of a bubblegum machine

I want to give up being a bullet
I've been a bullet too long

I want to be a good luck seed
lying idle in somebody's pocket
or some ordinary little stone
on the way to becoming an earring
or just lying there unknown
among a crowd of other ordinary stones

I want to give up being a bullet
I've been a bullet too long

The question is
Can you give up being a killer?

Victor Jara*

Victor Jara
Victor Jara

your name
bears the sound
of guitarra
your instrument of love

Victor Jara
Victor Jara

your name
bears the sound
of tierra
the earth you cherished
like your mother's songs

and how I wished
there was no need
for yet another poem
dedicated to hands
that still sing and bleed

how I wished
the silence of this poem
was shattered now
by bullets of love
from your guitar

Victor Jara
Victor guitarra
Victor tierra
Victor Jara
      Jara
      Jara
      Jar
         ah

* Chilean revolutionary singer murdered after the overthrow of Allende

Come From That Window Child

(for Pat Rodney & her children and the other thousands in whom
Walter Rodney* lives on)

Come from that window child
no use looking for daddy tonight
daddy not coming home tonight

Come from that window child
all you'll see is stars burning bright
you won't ever see daddy car light

Come from that window child
in your heart I know you asking why
in my heart too I wish the news was lie

Come from that window child
tonight I feel the darkness bleed
can't tell flower from seed

Come from that window child
to live for truth ain't no easy fight
when some believe power is their right

Come from that window child
a bomb blow up daddy car tonight
but daddy words still burning bright

Come from that window child
tonight you turn a man before your time
tonight you turn a man before your time

* Walter Rodney, a Guyanese historian revolutionary, author of *How
Europe Underdeveloped Africa*. Killed 13 June 1980 in Guyana.

Michael Smith*

Not since Rodney death
no Rodney murder/truer word/
dis dazed feeling
dis loss of breath
now a poet stoned to death

Mikey gone but how?

To believe/the fable of stone
aint no fable but true
To believe/in the hand that cast
the first stone/sin or no sin
To believe that we never learn
how not to wound ourselves/
intent on amputating
voice from voice/   stone the mirror
that stare too hard/   rub out the dub
of truth/   throw a stone at whoever
throw a poem/   to believe Babylon
to believe in the silence of stone
to believe it/believe it/believe it

But listen good Babylon
you can stone a poet
but he poem will live on
to heckle you

You better believe it/believe it/believe it

* A young Jamaican poet, most remembered for 'Mi Cyaan Believe It',
stoned to death outside the Jamaican Labour Party office in Stony Hill on
Wednesday 17 August 1983